Low-Fodmap Air Fryer Cookbook for Beginners

Low-Fodmap Air Fryer Cookbook for Beginners

The Ultimate Guide with Delicious, Gut-Friendly and Allergy-Friendly Air Fryer Recipes to Relieve the Symptoms of IBS and Other Digestive Disorders

Barey Bingle

TABLE OF CONTENTS

CHAPTER 7: DESSERTS RECIPES 099

CONCLUSION 114

INTRODUCTION

IBS and other digestive disorders are some of the most challenging to deal with emotionally because there is a certain amount of embarrassment which comes with digestion and when it goes wrong this is only intensified. The Low-Fodmap diet aim at reducing the ingestion of High-Fodmaps to allow the body to reach a level of normalcy. Throughout the course of this diet, each individual will discover how to create healthier eating habits.

Following the Low-Fodmap diet is actually more complicated than it sounds. There are certain things that you need to do to become successful while following the Low-Fodmap diet. The Air Fryer provides you with a way to eat healthier by providing you easy ways to prepare your Low-Fodmap recipes without losing the flavor of your meals.

The purpose of this cookbook is to increase your Low-Fodmap diet flexibility and variability. You will find a large number of awesome Air Fryer recipes which are low in Fodmaps. With so many tasty dishes to choose from, your daily food choice will soon be driven by delicious flavors. Get ready to enjoy a satisfying and symptom-free lifestyle.

CHAPTER 1: SNACK & APPETIZERS RECIPES

Yummy Chicken Dip

Preparation Time: 10 minutes
Cooking Time: 20 minutes
Serve: 6

Ingredients:

- 2 cups chicken, cooked and shredded
- 3/4 cup sour cream
- 1/4 tsp onion powder
- 8 oz cream cheese, softened
- 3 tbsp hot sauce
- 1/4 tsp garlic powder

Directions:

1.Preheat the air fryer to 325 F.
2.Add all ingredients in a large bowl and mix until well combined.
3.Transfer mixture in air fryer baking dish and place in the air fryer.
4.Cook chicken dip for 20 minutes.
5.Serve and enjoy.

Crab Mushrooms

Preparation Time: 10 minutes
Cooking Time: 8 minutes
Serve: 16

Ingredients:

- 16 mushrooms, clean and chop stems
- 1/4 tsp chili powder
- 1/4 tsp onion powder
- 1/4 cup mozzarella cheese, shredded
- 2 oz crab meat, chopped
- 8 oz cream cheese, softened
- 2 tsp garlic, minced
- 1/4 tsp pepper

Directions:

1. In a mixing bowl, mix together stems, chili powder, onion powder, pepper, cheese, crabmeat, cream cheese, and garlic until well combined.
2. Stuff mushrooms with bowl mixture and place into the air fryer basket.
3. Cook mushrooms at 370 F for 8 minutes.
4. Serve and enjoy.

Rangoon Crab Dip

Preparation Time: 10 minutes
Cooking Time: 16 minutes
Serve: 8

Ingredients:

- 2 cups crab meat
- 1 cup mozzarella cheese, shredded
- 1/2 tsp garlic powder
- 1/4 cup pimentos, drained and diced
- 1/4 tsp stevia
- 1/2 lemon juice
- 2 tsp coconut amino
- 2 tsp mayonnaise
- 8 oz cream cheese, softened
- 1 tbsp green onion
- 1/4 tsp pepper
- Salt

Directions:

1. Preheat the air fryer to 325 F.
2. Add all ingredients except half mozzarella cheese into the large bowl and mix until well combined.
3. Transfer bowl mixture into the air fryer baking dish and sprinkle with remaining mozzarella cheese.
4. Place into the air fryer and cook for 16 minutes.
5. Serve and enjoy.

Easy Carrot Dip

Preparation Time: 10 minutes
Cooking Time: 15 minutes
Serve: 6

Ingredients:

- 2 cups carrots, grated
- 1/4 tsp cayenne pepper
- 4 tbsp butter, melted
- 1 tbsp chives, chopped
- Pepper
- Salt

Directions:

1.Add all ingredients into the air fryer baking dish and stir until well combined.
2.Place dish in the air fryer and cook at 380 F for 15 minutes.
3.Transfer cook carrot mixture into the blender and blend until smooth.
4.Serve and enjoy.

Sesame Okra

Preparation Time: 10 minutes
Cooking Time: 4 minutes
Serve: 4

Ingredients:

- 11 oz okra, wash and chop
- 1 egg, lightly beaten
- 1 tsp sesame seeds
- 1 tbsp sesame oil
- 1/4 tsp pepper
- 1/2 tsp salt

Directions:

1. In a bowl, whisk together egg, pepper, and salt.
2. Add okra into the whisked egg. Sprinkle with sesame seeds.
3. Preheat the air fryer to 400 F.
4. Stir okra well. Spray air fryer basket with cooking spray.
5. Place okra pieces into the air fryer basket and cook for 4 minutes.
6. Serve and enjoy.

Perfect Crab Dip

Preparation Time: 5 minutes
Cooking Time: 7 minutes
Serve:4

Ingredients:

- 1 cup crabmeat
- 2 tbsp parsley, chopped
- 2 tbsp fresh lemon juice
- 2 tbsp hot sauce
- 1/2 cup green onion, sliced
- 2 cups cheese, grated
- 1/4 cup mayonnaise
- 1/4 tsp pepper
- 1/2 tsp salt

Directions:

1.In a 6-inch dish, mix together crabmeat, hot sauce, cheese, mayo, pepper, and salt.
2.Place dish in air fryer basket and cook dip at 400 F for 7 minutes.
3.Remove dish from air fryer.
4.Drizzle dip with lemon juice and garnish with parsley.
5.Serve and enjoy.

Sweet Potato Tots

Preparation Time: 10 minutes
Cooking Time: 31 minutes
Serve: 24

Ingredients:

- 2 sweet potatoes, peeled
- 1/2 tsp cajun seasoning
- Salt

Directions:

1. Add water in large pot and bring to boil. Add sweet potatoes in pot and boil for 15 minutes. Drain well.
2. Grated boil sweet potatoes into a large bowl using a grated.
3. Add cajun seasoning and salt in grated sweet potatoes and mix until well combined.
4. Spray air fryer basket with cooking spray.
5. Make small tot of sweet potato mixture and place in air fryer basket.
6. Cook at 400 F for 8 minutes. Turn tots to another side and cook for 8 minutes more.
7. Serve and enjoy.

Easy Jalapeno Poppers

Preparation Time: 10 minutes
Cooking Time: 13 minutes
Serve:5

Ingredients:

- 5 jalapeno peppers, slice in half and deseeded
- 2 tbsp salsa
- 4 oz goat cheese, crumbled
- 1/4 tsp chili powder
- 1/2 tsp garlic, minced
- Pepper
- Salt

Directions:

1.In a small bowl, mix together cheese, salsa, chili powder, garlic, pepper, and salt.
2.Spoon cheese mixture into each jalapeno halves and place in air fryer basket.
3.Cook jalapeno poppers at 350 F for 13 minutes.
4.Serve and enjoy.

Flavorful Pork Meatballs

Preparation Time: 10 minutes
Cooking Time: 10 minutes
Serve: 4

Ingredients:

- 2 eggs, lightly beaten
- 2 tbsp capers
- 1/2 lb ground pork
- 3 garlic cloves, minced
- 2 tbsp fresh mint, chopped
- 1/2 tbsp cilantro, chopped
- 2 tsp red pepper flakes, crushed
- 1 1/2 tbsp butter, melted
- 1 tsp kosher salt

Directions:

1.Preheat the air fryer to 395 F.
2.Add all ingredients into the mixing bowl and mix until well combined.
3.Spray air fryer basket with cooking spray.
4.Make small balls from meat mixture and place into the air fryer basket.
5.Cook meatballs for 10 minutes. Shake basket halfway through.
6.Serve and enjoy.

Veggie Cream Stuff Mushrooms

Preparation Time: 10 minutes
Cooking Time: 8 minutes
Serve: 12

Ingredients:

- 24 oz mushrooms, cut stems
- 1/2 cup sour cream
- 1 cup cheddar cheese, shredded
- 1 small carrot, diced
- 1/2 bell pepper, diced
- 1/2 onion, diced
- 2 bacon slices, diced

Directions:

1. Chop mushroom stems finely.
2. Spray pan with cooking spray and heat over medium heat.
3. Add chopped mushrooms, bacon, carrot, onion, and bell pepper into the pan and cook until tender.
4. Remove pan from heat. Add cheese and sour cream into the cooked vegetables and stir well.
5. Stuff vegetable mixture into the mushroom cap and place into the air fryer basket.
6. Cook mushrooms at 350 F for 8 minutes.
7. Serve and enjoy.

Jalapeno Cheese Dip

Preparation Time: 10 minutes
Cooking Time: 16 minutes
Serve: 6

Ingredients:

- 1 1/2 cup Monterey jack cheese, shredded
- 1 1/2 cup cheddar cheese, shredded
- 2 jalapeno pepper, minced
- 1 tsp garlic powder
- 1/3 cup sour cream
- 1/3 cup mayonnaise
- 8 oz cream cheese, softened
- 8 bacon slices, cooked and crumbled
- Pepper
- Salt

Directions:

1. Preheat the air fryer to 325 F.
2. Add all ingredients into the bowl and mix until combined.
3. Transfer bowl mixture into the air fryer baking dish and place in the air fryer and cook for 16 minutes.
4. Serve and enjoy.

Spinach Dip

Preparation Time: 10 minutes
Cooking Time: 40 minutes
Serve:8

Ingredients:

- 8 oz cream cheese, softened
- 1/4 tsp garlic powder
- 1/2 cup onion, minced
- 1/3 cup water chestnuts, drained and chopped
- 1 cup mayonnaise
- 1 cup parmesan cheese, grated
- 1 cup frozen spinach, thawed and squeeze out all liquid
- 1/2 tsp pepper

Directions:

1.Spray air fryer baking dish with cooking spray.
2.Add all ingredients into the bowl and mix until well combined.
3.Transfer bowl mixture into the prepared baking dish and place dish in air fryer basket.
4.Cook at 300 F for 35-40 minutes. After 20 minutes of cooking stir dip.
5.Serve and enjoy.

Shrimp Kabobs

Preparation Time: 10 minutes
Cooking Time: 8 minutes
Serve: 2

Ingredients:

- 1 cup shrimp
- 1 lime juice
- 1 garlic clove, minced
- 1/4 tsp pepper
- 1/8 tsp salt

Directions:

1. Preheat the air fryer to 350 F.
2. Add shrimp, lime juice, garlic, pepper, and salt into the bowl and toss well.
3. Thread shrimp onto the soaked wooden skewers and place into the air fryer basket.
4. Cook for 8 minutes. Turn halfway through.
5. Serve and enjoy.

Air Fried Cheese Sticks

Preparation Time: 10 minutes
Cooking Time: 8 minutes
Serve: 4 minutes

Ingredients:

- 6 mozzarella cheese sticks
- 1/4 tsp garlic powder
- 1 tsp Italian seasoning
- 1/3 cup almond flour
- 1/2 cup parmesan cheese, grated
- 1 large egg, lightly beaten
- 1/4 tsp sea salt

Directions:

1. In a small bowl, whisk the egg.
2. In a shallow bowl, mix together almond flour, parmesan cheese, Italian seasoning, garlic powder, and salt.
3. Dip mozzarella cheese stick in egg then coat with almond flour mixture and place on a plate. Place in refrigerator for 1 hour.
4. Spray air fryer basket with cooking spray.
5. Place prepared mozzarella cheese sticks into the air fryer basket and cook at 375 F for 8 minutes.
6. Serve and enjoy.

Shrimp Stuff Peppers

Preparation Time: 10 minutes
Cooking Time: 6 minutes
Serve: 6

Ingredients:

- 12 baby bell peppers, cut into halves
- 1 tbsp olive oil
- 1 tbsp fresh lemon juice
- ¼ cup basil pesto
- 1 lb shrimp, cooked
- ½ tsp red pepper flakes, crushed
- 2 tbsp parsley, chopped
- Pepper
- Salt

Directions:

1. In a bowl, mix together shrimp, parsley, red pepper flakes, basil pesto, lemon juice, oil, pepper, and salt.
2. Stuff shrimp mixture into the bell pepper halved and place into the air fryer basket.
3. Cook at 320 F for 6 minutes.
4. Serve and enjoy.

Zucchini Cheese Quiche

Preparation Time: 10 minutes
Cooking Time: 35 minutes
Serve: 6

Ingredients:

- 8 eggs
- 1 cup zucchini, shredded and squeezed
- 1 cup ham, cooked and diced
- 1/2 tsp dry mustard
- 1/2 cup heavy cream
- 1 cup cheddar cheese, shredded
- Pepper
- Salt

Directions:

1. Preheat the air fryer to 350 F.
2. Spray air fryer baking dish with cooking spray.
3. Combine ham, cheddar cheese, and zucchini in a baking dish.
4. In a bowl, whisk together eggs, heavy cream, and seasoning. Pour egg mixture over ham mixture.
5. Place dish in the air fryer and cook for 30-35 minutes.
6. Serve and enjoy.

Broccoli Muffins

Preparation Time: 10 minutes
Cooking Time: 24 minutes
Serve: 6

Ingredients:

- 2 large eggs
- 1 cup broccoli florets, chopped
- 1 cup unsweetened almond milk
- 2 cups almond flour
- 1 tsp baking powder
- 2 tbsp nutritional yeast
- 1/2 tsp sea salt

Directions:

1.Preheat the air fryer to 325 F.
2.Add all ingredients into the large bowl and mix until well combined.
3.Pour mixture into the silicone muffin molds and place into the air fryer basket.
4.Cook muffins for 20-24 minutes.
5.Serve and enjoy.

Lemon Dill Scallops

Preparation Time: 10 minutes
Cooking Time: 5 minutes
Serve: 4

Ingredients:

- 1 lb scallops
- 2 tsp olive oil
- 1 tsp dill, chopped
- 1 tbsp fresh lemon juice
- Pepper
- Salt

Directions:

1.Add scallops into the bowl and toss with oil, dill, lemon juice, pepper, and salt.
2.Add scallops into the air fryer basket and cook at 360 F for 5 minutes.
3.Serve and enjoy.

CHAPTER 2: BRUNCH RECIPES

Delicious Eggplant Hash

Preparation Time: 10 minutes
Cooking Time: 14 minutes
Serve: 4

Ingredients:

- 1 eggplant, chopped
- ¼ cup fresh mint, chopped
- ¼ cup basil, chopped
- 1 tsp Tabasco sauce
- ½ lb cherry tomatoes halved
- ½ cup olive oil
- Pepper
- Salt

Directions:

1. Heat oil in a pan over medium-high heat.
2. Add eggplant into the pan and cook for 3 minutes stir well and cook for 3 minutes more.
3. Transfer eggplant into the air fryer baking dish.
4. Add tomatoes in the same pan and cook for 1-2 minutes.
5. Transfer tomatoes in eggplant dish along with remaining ingredients and stir well.
6. Place dish in the air fryer and cook at 320 F for 6 minutes.
7. Serve and enjoy.

Egg Cups

Preparation Time: 10 minutes
Cooking Time: 18 minutes
Serve: 12

Ingredients:

- 12 eggs
- 4 oz cream cheese
- 12 bacon strips, uncooked
- 1/4 cup buffalo sauce
- 2/3 cup cheddar cheese, shredded
- Pepper
- Salt

Directions:

1. In a bowl, whisk together eggs, pepper, and salt.
2. Line each silicone muffin mold with one bacon strip.
3. Pour egg mixture into each muffin mold and place in the air fryer basket. (In batches)
4. Cook at 350 F for 8 minutes.
5. In another bowl, mix together cheddar cheese and cream cheese and microwave for 30 seconds. Add buffalo sauce and stir well.
6. Remove muffin molds from air fryer and add 2 tsp cheese mixture in the center of each egg cup.
7. Return muffin molds to the air fryer and cook for 10 minutes more.
8. Serve and enjoy.

Spicy Cauliflower Rice

Preparation Time: 10 minutes
Cooking Time: 22 minutes
Serve: 2

Ingredients:

- 1 cauliflower head, cut into florets
- 1/2 tsp cumin
- 1/2 tsp chili powder
- 6 onion spring, chopped
- 2 jalapenos, chopped
- 4 tbsp olive oil
- 1 zucchini, trimmed and cut into cubes
- 1/2 tsp paprika
- 1/2 tsp garlic powder
- 1/2 tsp cayenne pepper
- 1/2 tsp pepper
- 1/2 tsp salt

Directions:

1. Preheat the air fryer to 370 F.
2. Add cauliflower florets into the food processor and process until it looks like rice.
3. Transfer cauliflower rice into the air fryer baking pan and drizzle with half oil.
4. Place pan in the air fryer and cook for 12 minutes, stir halfway through.
5. Heat remaining oil in a small pan over medium heat.
6. Add zucchini and cook for 5-8 minutes.
7. Add onion and jalapenos and cook for 5 minutes.
8. Add spices and stir well. Set aside.
9. Add cauliflower rice in the zucchini mixture and stir well.
10. Serve and enjoy.

Almond Crust Chicken

Preparation Time: 10 minutes
Cooking Time: 25 minutes
Serve: 2

Ingredients:

- 2 chicken breasts, skinless and boneless
- 1 tbsp Dijon mustard
- 2 tbsp mayonnaise
- ¼ cup almonds
- Pepper
- Salt

Directions:

1. Add almond into the food processor and process until finely ground. Transfer almonds on a plate and set aside.
2. Mix together mustard and mayonnaise and spread over chicken.
3. Coat chicken with almond and place into the air fryer basket and cook at 350 F for 25 minutes.
4. Serve and enjoy.

Breakfast Casserole

Preparation Time: 10 minutes
Cooking Time: 28 minutes
Serve: 4

Ingredients:

- 2 eggs
- 4 egg whites
- 4 tsp pine nuts, minced
- 2/3 cup chicken broth
- 1 lb Italian sausage
- 1/4 cup roasted red pepper, sliced
- 1/4 cup pesto sauce
- 2/3 cup parmesan cheese, grated
- 1/8 tsp pepper
- 1/4 tsp sea salt

Directions:

1. Preheat the air fryer to 370 F.
2. Spray air fryer pan with cooking spray and set aside.
3. Heat another pan over medium heat. Add sausage in a pan and cook until golden brown.
4. Once cooked then drain excess oil and spread it into the prepared pan.
5. Whisk remaining ingredients except pine nuts in a bowl and pour over sausage.
6. Place pan in the air fryer and cook for 25-28 minutes.
7. Top with pine nuts and serve.

Vegetable Egg Cups

Preparation Time:10 minutes
Cooking Time:20 minutes
Serve:4

Ingredients:

- 4 eggs
- 1 tbsp cilantro, chopped
- 4 tbsp half and half
- 1 cup cheddar cheese, shredded
- 1 cup vegetables, diced
- Pepper
- Salt

Directions:

1.Spray four ramekins with cooking spray and set aside.
2.In a mixing bowl, whisk eggs with cilantro, half and half, vegetables, 1/2 cup cheese, pepper, and salt.
3.Pour egg mixture into the four ramekins.
4.Place ramekins in air fryer basket and cook at 300 F for 12 minutes.
5.Top with remaining 1/2 cup cheese and cook for 2 minutes more at 400 F.
6.Serve and enjoy.

Spinach Frittata

Preparation Time: 5 minutes
Cooking Time: 8 minutes
Serve: 1

Ingredients:

- 3 eggs
- 1 cup spinach, chopped
- 1 small onion, minced
- 2 tbsp mozzarella cheese, grated
- Pepper
- Salt

Directions:

1. Preheat the air fryer to 350 F.
2. Spray air fryer pan with cooking spray.
3. In a bowl, whisk eggs with remaining ingredients until well combined.
4. Pour egg mixture into the prepared pan and place pan in the air fryer basket.
5. Cook frittata for 8 minutes or until set.
6. Serve and enjoy.

Asparagus Frittata

Preparation Time: 10 minutes
Cooking Time: 10 minutes
Serve: 4

Ingredients:

- 6 eggs
- 3 mushrooms, sliced
- 10 asparagus, chopped
- 1/4 cup half and half
- 2 tsp butter, melted
- 1 cup mozzarella cheese, shredded
- 1 tsp pepper
- 1 tsp salt

Directions:

1. Toss mushrooms and asparagus with melted butter and add into the air fryer basket.
2. Cook mushrooms and asparagus at 350 F for 5 minutes. Shake basket twice.
3. Meanwhile, in a bowl, whisk together eggs, half and half, pepper, and salt.
4. Transfer cook mushrooms and asparagus into the air fryer baking dish.
5. Pour egg mixture over mushrooms and asparagus.
6. Place dish in the air fryer and cook at 350 F for 5 minutes or until eggs are set.
7. Slice and serve.

Healthy Squash

Preparation Time: 10 minutes
Cooking Time: 25 minutes
Serve: 4

Ingredients:

- 2 lbs yellow squash, cut into half-moons
- 1 tsp Italian seasoning
- ¼ tsp pepper
- 1 tbsp olive oil
- ¼ tsp salt

Directions:

1. Add all ingredients into the large bowl and toss well.
2. Preheat the air fryer to 400 F.
3. Add squash mixture into the air fryer basket and cook for 10 minutes.
4. Shake basket and cook for another 10 minutes.
5. Shake once again and cook for 5 minutes more.

-

Breakfast Egg Tomato

Preparation Time: 10 minutes
Cooking Time: 24 minutes
Serve: 2

Ingredients:

- 2 eggs
- 2 large fresh tomatoes
- 1 tsp fresh parsley
- Pepper
- Salt

Directions:

1.Preheat the air fryer to 325 F.
2.Cut off the top of a tomato and spoon out the tomato innards.
3.Break the egg in each tomato and place in air fryer basket and cook for 24 minutes.
4.Season with parsley, pepper, and salt.
5.Serve and enjoy.

-

CHAPTER 3: POULTRY RECIPES

Turkey Meatballs

Preparation Time: 10 minutes
Cooking Time: 12 minutes
Serve: 4

Ingredients:

- 1 lb ground turkey
- 2 garlic cloves, minced
- ¼ cup carrots, grated
- 1 egg, lightly beaten
- 2 tbsp coconut flour
- 2 green onion, chopped
- ¼ cup celery, chopped
- Pepper
- Salt

Directions:

1. Spray air fryer basket with cooking spray.
2. Preheat the air fryer to 400 F.
3. Add all ingredients into the large bowl and mix until well combined.
4. Make balls from meat mixture and place into the air fryer basket and cook for 12 minutes. Turn halfway through.
5. Serve and enjoy.

Asain Chicken Wings

Preparation Time: 10 minutes
Cooking Time: 30 minutes
Serve: 2

Ingredients:

- 4 chicken wings
- 3/4 tbsp Chinese spice
- 1 tbsp soy sauce
- 1 tsp mixed spice
- Pepper
- Salt

Directions:

1.Add chicken wings into the bowl. Add remaining ingredients and toss to coat.
2.Transfer chicken wings into the air fryer basket.
3.Cook at 350 f for 15 minutes.
4.Turn chicken to another side and cook for 15 minutes more.
5.Serve and enjoy.

Quick & Simple Chicken Breast

Preparation Time: 10 minutes
Cooking Time: 22 minutes
Serve: 4

Ingredients:

- 4 chicken breasts, skinless and boneless
- 1/2 tsp dried oregano
- 1/2 tsp dried basil
- 1/2 tsp dried thyme
- 1/2 tsp garlic powder
- 2 tbsp olive oil
- 1/8 tsp pepper
- 1/2 tsp salt

Directions:

1. In a small bowl, mix together olive oil, oregano, basil, thyme, garlic powder, pepper, and salt.
2. Rub herb oil mixture all over chicken breasts.
3. Spray air fryer basket with cooking spray.
4. Place chicken in air fryer basket and cook at 360 F for 10 minutes.
5. Turn chicken to another side and cook for 8-12 minutes more or until the internal temperature of chicken reaches at 165 F.
6. Serve and enjoy.

-

Dijon Turkey Drumstick

Preparation Time: 10 minutes
Cooking Time: 28 minutes
Serve: 2

Ingredients:

- 4 turkey drumsticks
- 1/3 tsp paprika
- 1/3 cup sherry wine
- 1/3 cup coconut milk
- 1/2 tbsp ginger, minced
- 2 tbsp Dijon mustard
- Pepper
- Salt

Directions:

1. Add all ingredients into the large bowl and stir to coat. Place in refrigerator for 2 hours.
2. Spray air fryer basket with cooking spray.
3. Place marinated turkey drumsticks into the air fryer basket and cook at 380 F for 28 minutes. Turn halfway through.
4. Serve and enjoy.

Garlic Herb Chicken Breasts

Preparation Time: 10 minutes
Cooking Time: 15 minutes
Serve: 5

Ingredients:

- 2 lbs chicken breasts, skinless and boneless
- 4 garlic cloves, minced
- ¼ cup yogurt
- ¼ cup mayonnaise
- 2 tsp garlic herb seasoning
- 1/2 tsp onion powder
- ¼ tsp salt

Directions:

1. Preheat the air fryer to 380 F.
2. In a small bowl, mix together mayonnaise, seasoning, onion powder, garlic, and yogurt.
3. Brush chicken with mayo mixture and season with salt.
4. Spray air fryer basket with cooking spray.
5. Place chicken into the air fryer basket and cook for 15 minutes.
6. Serve and enjoy.

-

Quick & Easy Meatballs

Preparation Time: 10 minutes
Cooking Time: 10 minutes
Serve: 4

Ingredients:

- 1 lb ground chicken
- 1 egg, lightly beaten
- 1/2 cup mozzarella cheese, shredded
- 1 1/2 tbsp taco seasoning
- 3 garlic cloves, minced
- 3 tbsp fresh parsley, chopped
- 1 small onion, minced
- Pepper
- Salt

Directions:

1.Add all ingredients into the large mixing bowl and mix until well combined.
2.Make small balls from mixture and place in the air fryer basket.
3.Cook meatballs for 10 minutes at 400 F.
4.Serve and enjoy.

Indian Chicken Tenders

Preparation Time: 10 minutes
Cooking Time: 15 minutes
Serve: 4

Ingredients:

- 1 lb chicken tenders, cut in half
- ¼ cup parsley, chopped
- 1/2 tbsp garlic, minced
- 1/2 tbsp ginger, minced
- ¼ cup yogurt
- 3/4 tsp paprika
- 1 tsp garam masala
- 1 tsp turmeric
- 1/2 tsp cayenne pepper
- 1 tsp salt

Directions:

1. Preheat the air fryer to 350 F.
2. Add all ingredients into the large bowl and mix well. Place in refrigerator for 30 minutes.
3. Spray air fryer basket with cooking spray.
4. Add marinated chicken into the air fryer basket and cook for 10 minutes.
5. Turn chicken to another side and cook for 5 minutes more.
6. Serve and enjoy.

Easy & Spicy Chicken Wings

Preparation Time: 10 minutes
Cooking Time: 25 minutes
Serve: 2

Ingredients:

- 1 lb chicken wings
- 1/2 tsp pepper
- 1/2 tsp salt
- For sauce:
- 1/2 tbsp sesame oil
- 1/2 tbsp mayonnaise
- 1 tbsp gochujang
- 1/2 tbsp garlic, minced
- 1.2 tbsp ginger, minced

Directions:

1. Preheat the air fryer to 400 F.
2. Add chicken wings into the air fryer basket and season with pepper and salt and cook for 20 minutes.
3. Meanwhile, in a bowl mix together all sauce ingredients.
4. Toss chicken wings with sauce and cook for 5 minutes more.
5. Serve and enjoy.

Chicken Fajita Casserole

Preparation Time: 10 minutes
Cooking Time: 12 minutes
Serve: 4

Ingredients:

- 1 lb cooked chicken, shredded
- 1 onion, sliced
- 1 bell pepper, sliced
- 1/3 cup mayonnaise
- 7 oz cream cheese
- 7 oz cheese, shredded
- 2 tbsp tex-mex seasoning
- Pepper
- Salt

Directions:

1. Preheat the air fryer to 370 F.
2. Spray air fryer baking dish with cooking spray.
3. Mix all ingredients except 2 oz shredded cheese in a prepared dish.
4. Spread remaining cheese on top.
5. Place dish in the air fryer and cook for 12 minutes.
6. Serve and enjoy.

Tasty Caribbean Chicken

Preparation Time: 10 minutes
Cooking Time: 10 minutes
Serve: 8

Ingredients:

- 3 lbs chicken thigh, skinless and boneless
- 1 tbsp coriander powder
- 3 tbsp coconut oil, melted
- ½ tsp ground nutmeg
- ½ tsp ground ginger
- 1 tbsp cayenne
- 1 tbsp cinnamon
- Pepper
- Salt

Directions:

1. In a small bowl, mix together all spices and rub all over the chicken.
2. Spray air fryer basket with cooking spray.
3. Place chicken into the air fryer basket and cook at 390 F for 10 minutes.
4. Serve and enjoy.

Curried Drumsticks

Preparation Time: 10 minutes
Cooking Time: 22 minutes
Serve: 2

Ingredients:

- 2 turkey drumsticks
- 1/3 cup coconut milk
- 1 1/2 tbsp ginger, minced
- 1/4 tsp cayenne pepper
- 2 tbsp red curry paste
- 1/4 tsp pepper
- 1 tsp kosher salt

Directions:

1. Add all ingredients into the bowl and stir to coat. Place in refrigerator for overnight.
2. Spray air fryer basket with cooking spray.
3. Place marinated drumsticks into the air fryer basket and cook at 390 F for 22 minutes.
4. Serve and enjoy.

Korean Chicken Tenders

Preparation Time: 10 minutes
Cooking Time: 10 minutes
Serve: 3

Ingredients:

- 12 oz chicken tenders, skinless and boneless
- 2 tbsp green onion, chopped
- 3 garlic cloves, chopped
- 2 tsp sesame seeds, toasted
- 1 tbsp ginger, grated
- 1/4 cup sesame oil
- 1/2 cup soy sauce
- 1/4 tsp pepper

Directions:

1. Slide chicken tenders onto the skewers.
2. In a large bowl, mix together green onion, garlic, sesame seeds, ginger, sesame oil, soy sauce, and pepper.
3. Add chicken skewers into the bowl and coat well with marinade. Place in refrigerator for overnight.
4. Preheat the air fryer to 390 F.
5. Place marinated chicken skewers into the air fryer basket and cook for 10 minutes.

-

Mediterranean Chicken

Preparation Time: 10 minutes
Cooking Time: 35 minutes
Serve: 6

Ingredients:

- 4 lbs whole chicken, cut into pieces
- 2 tsp ground sumac
- 2 garlic cloves, minced
- 2 lemons, sliced
- 2 tbsp olive oil
- 1 tsp lemon zest
- 2 tsp kosher salt

Directions:

1. Rub chicken with oil, sumac, lemon zest, and salt. Place in the refrigerator for 2-3 hours.
2. Add lemon sliced into the air fryer basket top with marinated chicken.
3. Cook at 350 for 35 minutes.
4. Serve and enjoy.

-

Classic Chicken Wings

Preparation Time: 10 minutes
Cooking Time: 40 minutes
Serve: 4

Ingredients:

- 2 lbs chicken wings
For sauce:
- 1/4 tsp Tabasco
- 1/4 tsp Worcestershire sauce
- 6 tbsp butter, melted
- 12 oz hot sauce

Directions:

1. Spray air fryer basket with cooking spray.
2. Add chicken wings in air fryer basket and cook for 25 minutes at 380 F. Shake basket after every 5 minutes.
3. After 25 minutes turn temperature to 400 F and cook for 10-15 minutes more.
4. Meanwhile, in a large bowl, mix together all sauce ingredients.
5. Add cooked chicken wings in a sauce bowl and toss well to coat.
6. Serve and enjoy.

CHAPTER 4: BEEF PORK & LAMB RECIPES

Crisp Pork Chops

Preparation Time: 10 minutes
Cooking Time: 12 minutes
Serve: 6

Ingredients:

- 1 1/2 lbs pork chops, boneless
- 1 tsp paprika
- 1 tsp creole seasoning
- 1 tsp garlic powder
- 1/4 cup parmesan cheese, grated
- 1/3 cup almond flour

Directions:

1. Preheat the air fryer to 360 F.
2. Add all ingredients except pork chops in a zip-lock bag.
3. Add pork chops in the bag. Seal bag and shake well to coat pork chops.
4. Remove pork chops from zip-lock bag and place in the air fryer basket.
5. Cook pork chops for 10-12 minutes.
6. Serve and enjoy.

Lamb Meatballs

Preparation Time: 10 minutes
Cooking Time: 14 minutes
Serve: 8

Ingredients:

- 1 egg, lightly beaten
- 1 lb ground lamb
- ¼ tsp bay leaf, crushed
- 1 tsp ground coriander
- ¼ tsp cayenne pepper
- ¼ tsp turmeric
- 1 onion, chopped
- 2 garlic cloves, minced
- ¼ tsp pepper
- 1 tsp salt

Directions:

1. Preheat the air fryer to 400 F.
2. Spray air fryer basket with cooking spray.
3. Add all ingredients into the large bowl and mix until well combined.
4. Make small balls from meat mixture and place into the air fryer basket and cook for 14 minutes. Shake basket twice while cooking.
5. Serve and enjoy.

Lamb Rack

Preparation Time: 10 minutes
Cooking Time: 30 minutes
Serve: 6

Ingredients:

- 1 egg, lightly beaten
- 1 tbsp fresh thyme, chopped
- 1 3/4 lbs rack of lamb
- 1 tbsp fresh rosemary, chopped
- 1 tbsp olive oil
- 2 garlic cloves, chopped
- Pepper
- Salt

Directions:

1.Mix together oil and garlic.
2.Brush oil and garlic mixture over the rack of lamb. Season with pepper and salt.
3.Preheat the air fryer to 210 F.
4.Mix together thyme and rosemary.
5.Coat lamb with egg then with herb mixture.
6.Place lamb rack in the air fryer basket and cook for 25 minutes.
7.Turn temperature to 390 F and cook for 5 minutes more.
8.Serve and enjoy.

Meatloaf

Preparation Time: 10 minutes
Cooking Time: 15 minutes
Serve: 4

Ingredients:

- 1 lb ground beef
- 1/4 tsp cinnamon
- 1 tbsp ginger, minced
- 1/4 cup fresh cilantro, chopped
- 1 cup onion, diced
- 2 eggs, lightly beaten
- 1 tsp cayenne
- 1 tsp turmeric
- 1 tsp garam masala
- 1 tbsp garlic, minced
- 1 tsp salt

Directions:

1.Add all ingredients into the large bowl and mix until combined.
2.Transfer meat mixture into the silicone meatloaf pan.
3.Place in the air fryer and cook at 360 F for 15 minutes.
4.Slice and serve.

-

Pork Strips

Preparation Time: 10 minutes
Cooking Time: 10 minutes
Serve: 2

Ingredients:

- 4 pork loin chops
- 1 tbsp swerve
- 1 tbsp soy sauce
- 1/8 tsp ground ginger
- 1 garlic clove, chopped
- 1/2 tsp balsamic vinegar

Directions:

1.Tenderize meat and season with pepper and salt.
2.In a bowl, mix together sweetener, soy sauce, and vinegar. Add ginger and garlic and set aside.
3.Add pork chops into the marinade mixture and marinate for 2 hours.
4.Preheat the air fryer to 350 F.
5.Add marinated meat into the air fryer and cook for 5 minutes on each side.
6.Cut into strips and serve.

Asian Beef

Preparation Time: 10 minutes
Cooking Time: 20 minutes
Serve: 4

Ingredients:

- 1 lb beef tips, sliced
- 1/4 cup green onion, chopped
- 2 tbsp garlic, minced
- 2 tbsp sesame oil
- 1 tbsp fish sauce
- 2 tbsp coconut aminos
- 1 tsp xanthan gum
- 2 red chili peppers, sliced
- 2 tbsp water
- 1 tbsp ginger, sliced

Directions:

1. Spray air fryer basket with cooking spray.
2. Toss beef and xanthan gum together.
3. Add beef into the air fryer basket and cook at 390F for 20 minutes. Toss halfway through.
4. Meanwhile, in a saucepan add remaining ingredients except for green onion and heat over low heat.
5. When sauce begins to boiling then remove from heat.
6. Add cooked meat into the saucepan and stir to coat. Let sit in for 5 minutes.
7. Garnish with green onion and serve.

Broccoli Beef

Preparation Time: 10 minutes
Cooking Time: 12 minutes
Serve: 5

Ingredients:

- 1 lb round steak, cut into strips
- 1 lb broccoli florets
- 5 drops liquid stevia
- 1 tsp soy sauce
- 1/3 cup sherry
- 2 tsp sesame oil
- 1/3 cup oyster sauce
- 1 garlic clove, minced
- 1 tbsp ginger, sliced
- 1 tsp arrowroot powder
- 1 tbsp olive oil

Directions:

1. In a small bowl, combine together oyster sauce, stevia, soy sauce, sherry, arrowroot, and sesame oil.
2. Add broccoli and meat in a large bowl.
3. Pour oyster sauce mixture over meat and broccoli and toss well. Place in the fridge for 60 minutes.
4. Add marinated meat broccoli to the air fryer basket. Drizzle with olive oil and sprinkle with ginger and garlic.
5. Cook at 360 F for 12 minutes.
6. Serve and enjoy.

Meatloaf Sliders

Preparation Time: 10 minutes
Cooking Time: 10 minutes
Serve: 8

Ingredients:

- 1 lb ground beef
- 1/2 tsp dried tarragon
- 1 tsp Italian seasoning
- 1 tbsp Worcestershire sauce
- 1/4 cup ketchup
- 1/4 cup coconut flour
- 1/2 cup almond flour
- 1 garlic clove, minced
- 1/4 cup onion, chopped
- 2 eggs, lightly beaten
- 1/4 tsp pepper
- 1/2 tsp sea salt

Directions:

1. Add all ingredients into the mixing bowl and mix until well combined.
2. Make the equal shape of patties from mixture and place on a plate. Place in refrigerator for 10 minutes.
3. Spray air fryer basket with cooking spray.
4. Preheat the air fryer to 360 F.
5. Place prepared patties in air fryer basket and cook for 10 minutes.
6. Serve and enjoy.

Juicy & Tender Steak

Preparation Time: 10 minutes
Cooking Time: 12 minutes
Serve: 2

Ingredients:

- 2 rib-eye steak
- 3 tbsp fresh parsley, chopped
- 1 stick butter, softened
- 1 1/2 tsp Worcestershire sauce
- 3 garlic cloves, minced
- Pepper
- Salt

Directions:

1. In a bowl, mix together butter, Worcestershire sauce, garlic, parsley, and salt and place in the refrigerator.
2. Preheat the air fryer to 400 F.
3. Season steak with pepper and salt.
4. Place seasoned steak in the air fryer and cook for 12 minutes. Turn halfway through.
5. Remove steak from air fryer and top with butter mixture.
6. Serve and enjoy.

Steak Fajitas

Preparation Time: 10 minutes
Cooking Time: 15 minutes
Serve: 6

Ingredients:

- 1 lb steak, sliced
- 1 tbsp olive oil
- 1 tbsp fajita seasoning, gluten-free
- 1/2 cup onion, sliced
- 3 bell peppers, sliced

Directions:

1. Line air fryer basket with aluminum foil.
2. Add all ingredients large bowl and toss until well coated.
3. Transfer fajita mixture into the air fryer basket and cook at 390 F for 5 minutes.
4. Toss well and cook for 5-10 minutes more.
5. Serve and enjoy.

Garlic Pork Chops

Preparation Time: 5 minutes
Cooking Time: 20 minutes
Serve: 5

Ingredients:

- 2 lbs pork chops
- 2 tbsp garlic, minced
- 1 tbsp fresh parsley
- 2 tbsp olive oil
- 2 tbsp fresh lemon juice
- Pepper
- Salt

Directions:

1. In a small bowl, mix together garlic, parsley, oil, and lemon juice.
2. Season pork chops with pepper and salt.
3. Rub garlic mixture over the pork chops and allow to marinate for 30 minutes.
4. Add marinated pork chops into the air fryer and cook at 400 F for 10 minutes.
5. Turn pork chops to another side and cook for 10 minutes more.
6. Serve and enjoy.

Asian Pork

Preparation Time: 10 minutes
Cooking Time: 15 minutes
Serve: 4

Ingredients:

- 1 lb pork shoulder, boneless and cut into 1/2 inch sliced
- 3 tbsp green onions, sliced
- 3 garlic cloves, minced
- 1 tbsp ginger, minced
- 2 tbsp red pepper paste
- 1 onion, sliced
- 1 tbsp sesame seeds
- 3/4 tsp cayenne pepper
- 1 tbsp sesame oil
- 1 tbsp rice wine

Directions:

1.Add all ingredients into the bowl and mix well and place in the refrigerator for 1 hour.
2.Place marinated meat and onion slices into the air fryer.
3.Cook at 400 F for 15 minutes. Toss halfway through.
4.Serve and enjoy.

Easy Burger Patties

Preparation Time: 10 minutes
Cooking Time: 45 minutes
Serve: 4

Ingredients:

- 10 oz ground beef
- 1 tsp dried basil
- 1 tsp mustard
- 1 tsp tomato paste
- 1 oz cheddar cheese
- 1 tsp mixed herbs
- 1 tsp garlic puree
- Pepper
- Salt

Directions:

1. Add all ingredients into the large bowl and mix until combined.
2. Spray air fryer basket with cooking spray.
3. Make patties from meat mixture and place into the air fryer basket.
4. Cook at 390 F for 25 minutes then turn patties to another side and cook at 350 F for 20 minutes more.
5. Serve and enjoy.

Meatballs

Preparation Time: 10 minutes
Cooking Time: 8 minutes
Serve: 10

Ingredients:

- 5 oz ground beef
- 1 tbsp fresh oregano, chopped
- 2 oz feta cheese, crumbled
- 2 tbsp almond flour
- 1/4 tsp garlic powder
- 1/4 tsp paprika
- Pepper
- Salt

Directions:

1.Preheat the air fryer to 390 F.
2.Add all ingredients into the bowl and mix until well combined.
3.Make small balls from meat mixture and place into the air fryer basket.
4.Cook for 8 minutes.
5.Serve and enjoy.

CHAPTER 5: SEAFOOD & FISH RECIPES

Shrimp with Veggie

Preparation Time: 10 minutes
Cooking Time: 20 minutes
Serve: 4

Ingredients:

- 50 small shrimp
- 1 tbsp Cajun seasoning
- 1 bag of frozen mix vegetables
- 1 tbsp olive oil

Directions:

1. Line air fryer basket with aluminum foil.
2. Add all ingredients into the large mixing bowl and toss well.
3. Transfer shrimp and vegetable mixture into the air fryer basket and cook at 350 F for 10 minutes.
4. Toss well and cook for 10 minutes more.
5. Serve and enjoy.

Air Fried King Prawns

Preparation Time: 10 minutes
Cooking Time: 6 minutes
Serve: 4

Ingredients:

- 12 king prawns
- 1 tbsp vinegar
- 1 tbsp ketchup
- 3 tbsp mayonnaise
- 1/2 tsp pepper
- 1 tsp chili powder
- 1 tsp red chili flakes
- 1/2 tsp sea salt

Directions:

1. Preheat the air fryer to 350 F.
2. Spray air fryer basket with cooking spray.
3. Add prawns, chili flakes, chili powder, pepper, and salt to the bowl and toss well.
4. Transfer shrimp to the air fryer basket and cook for 6 minutes.
5. In a small bowl, mix together mayonnaise, ketchup, and vinegar.
6. Serve with mayo mixture and enjoy.

-

Salmon Patties

Preparation Time: 10 minutes
Cooking Time: 7 minutes
Serve: 2

Ingredients:

- 8 oz salmon fillet, minced
- 1 lemon, sliced
- 1/2 tsp garlic powder
- 1 egg, lightly beaten
- 1/8 tsp salt

Directions:

1. Add all ingredients except lemon slices into the bowl and mix until well combined.
2. Spray air fryer basket with cooking spray.
3. Place lemon slice into the air fryer basket.
4. Make the equal shape of patties from salmon mixture and place on top of lemon slices into the air fryer basket.
5. Cook at 390 F for 7 minutes.
6. Serve and enjoy.

Tuna Patties

Preparation Time: 10 minutes
Cooking Time: 10 minutes
Serve: 2

Ingredients:

- 2 cans tuna
- 1/2 lemon juice
- 1/2 tsp onion powder
- 1 tsp garlic powder
- 1/2 tsp dried dill
- 1 1/2 tbsp mayonnaise
- 1 1/2 tbsp almond flour
- 1/4 tsp pepper
- 1/4 tsp salt

Directions:

1. Preheat the air fryer to 400 F.
2. Add all ingredients in a mixing bowl and mix until well combined.
3. Spray air fryer basket with cooking spray.
4. Make four patties from mixture and place in the air fryer basket.
5. Cook patties for 10 minutes at 400 F if you want crispier patties then cook for 3 minutes more.
6. Serve and enjoy.

Fish Packets

Preparation Time: 10 minutes
Cooking Time: 15 minutes
Serve: 2

Ingredients:

- 2 cod fish fillets
- 1/2 tsp dried tarragon
- 1/2 cup bell peppers, sliced
- 1/4 cup celery, cut into julienne
- 1/2 cup carrots, cut into julienne
- 1 tbsp olive oil
- 1 tbsp lemon juice
- 2 pats butter, melted
- Pepper
- Salt

Directions:

1. In a bowl, mix together butter, lemon juice, tarragon, and salt. Add vegetables and toss well. Set aside.
2. Take two parchments paper pieces to fold vegetables and fish.
3. Spray fish with cooking spray and season with pepper and salt.
4. Place a fish fillet on each parchment paper piece and top with vegetables.
5. Fold parchment paper around the fish and vegetables.
6. Place veggie fish packets into the air fryer basket and cook at 350 F for 15 minutes.
7. Serve and enjoy.

Pesto Salmon

Preparation Time: 10 minutes
Cooking Time: 16 minutes
Serve: 2

Ingredients:

- 2 salmon fillets
- 1/4 cup parmesan cheese, grated
- For pesto:
- 1/4 cup pine nuts
- 1/4 cup olive oil
- 1 1/2 cups fresh basil leaves
- 2 garlic cloves, peeled and chopped
- 1/4 cup parmesan cheese, grated
- 1/2 tsp pepper
- 1/2 tsp salt

Directions:

1. Add all pesto ingredients to the blender and blend until smooth.
2. Preheat the air fryer to 370 F.
3. Spray air fryer basket with cooking spray.
4. Place salmon fillet into the air fryer basket and spread 2 tablespoons of the pesto on each salmon fillet.
5. Sprinkle grated cheese on top of the pesto.
6. Cook salmon for 16 minutes.
7. Serve and enjoy.

Creamy Shrimp

Preparation Time: 10 minutes
Cooking Time: 8 minutes
Serve: 4

Ingredients:

- 1 lb shrimp, peeled
- 1 tbsp garlic, minced
- 1 tbsp tomato ketchup
- 3 tbsp mayonnaise
- 1/2 tsp paprika
- 1 tsp sriracha
- 1/2 tsp salt

Directions:

1. In a bowl, mix together mayonnaise, paprika, sriracha, garlic, ketchup, and salt. Add shrimp and stir well.
2. Add shrimp mixture into the air fryer baking dish and place in the air fryer.
3. Cook at 325 F for 8 minutes. Stir halfway through.
4. Serve and enjoy.

Lemon Crab Patties

Preparation Time: 10 minutes
Cooking Time: 10 minutes
Serve: 4

Ingredients:

- 1 egg
- 12 oz crabmeat
- 2 green onion, chopped
- 1/4 cup mayonnaise
- 1 cup almond flour
- 1 tsp old bay seasoning
- 1 tsp red pepper flakes
- 1 tbsp fresh lemon juice

Directions:

1. Preheat the air fryer to 400 F.
2. Spray air fryer basket with cooking spray.
3. Add 1/2 almond flour into the mixing bowl.
4. Add remaining ingredients and mix until well combined.
5. Make patties from mixture and coat with remaining almond flour and place into the air fryer basket.
6. Cook patties for 5 minutes then turn to another side and cook for 5 minutes more.
7. Serve and enjoy.

Lemon Butter Salmon

Preparation Time: 10 minutes
Cooking Time: 11 minutes
Serve: 2

Ingredients:

- 2 salmon fillets
- 1/2 tsp olive oil
- 2 tsp garlic, minced
- 2 tbsp butter
- 2 tbsp fresh lemon juice
- 1/4 cup white wine
- Pepper
- Salt

Directions:

1. Preheat the air fryer to 350 F.
2. Spray air fryer basket with cooking spray.
3. Season salmon with pepper and salt and place into the air fryer basket and cook for 6 minutes.
4. Meanwhile, in a saucepan, add remaining ingredients and heat over low heat for 4-5 minutes.
5. Place cooked salmon on serving dish then pour prepared sauce over salmon.
6. Serve and enjoy.

Chili Garlic Shrimp

Preparation Time: 10 minutes
Cooking Time: 7 minutes
Serve: 4

Ingredients:

- 1 lb shrimp, peeled and deveined
- 1 tbsp olive oil
- 1 lemon, sliced
- 1 red chili pepper, sliced
- 1/2 tsp garlic powder
- Pepper
- Salt

Directions:

1.Preheat the air fryer to 400 F.
2.Spray air fryer basket with cooking spray.
3.Add all ingredients into the bowl and toss well.
4.Add shrimp into the air fryer basket and cook for 5 minutes. Shake basket twice.
5.Serve and enjoy.

Cheesy Crab Dip

Preparation Time: 10 minutes
Cooking Time: 7 minutes
Serve: 4

Ingredients:

- 1 cup crabmeat, cooked
- 2 tbsp fresh parsley, chopped
- 2 tbsp fresh lemon juice
- 2 cups Jalapeno jack cheese, grated
- 2 tbsp hot sauce
- 1/2 cup green onions, sliced
- 1/4 cup mayonnaise
- 1 tsp pepper
- 1/2 tsp salt

Directions:

1. Add all ingredients except parsley and lemon juice in air fryer baking dish and stir well.
2. Place dish in the air fryer basket and cook at 400 F for 7 minutes.
3. Add parsley and lemon juice. Mix well.
4. Serve and enjoy.

Delicious Crab Cakes

Preparation Time: 10 minutes
Cooking Time: 10 minutes
Serve: 4

Ingredients:

- 8 oz crab meat
- 2 tbsp butter, melted
- 2 tsp Dijon mustard
- 1 tbsp mayonnaise
- 1 egg, lightly beaten
- 1/2 tsp old bay seasoning
- 1 green onion, sliced
- 2 tbsp parsley, chopped
- 1/4 cup almond flour
- 1/4 tsp pepper
- 1/2 tsp salt

Directions:

1.Add all ingredients except butter in a mixing bowl and mix until well combined.
2.Make four equal shapes of patties from mixture and place on parchment lined plate.
3.Place plate in the fridge for 30 minutes.
4.Spray air fryer basket with cooking spray.
5.Brush melted butter on both sides of crab patties.
6.Place crab patties in air fryer basket and cook for 10 minutes at 350 F.
7.Turn patties halfway through.
8.Serve and enjoy.

Perfect Salmon Fillets

Preparation Time: 10 minutes
Cooking Time: 15 minutes
Serve: 2

Ingredients:

- 2 salmon fillets
- 1/2 tsp garlic powder
- 1/4 cup plain yogurt
- 1 tsp fresh lemon juice
- 1 tbsp fresh dill, chopped
- 1 lemon, sliced
- Pepper
- Salt

Directions:

1. Place lemon slices into the air fryer basket.
2. Season salmon with pepper and salt and place on top of lemon slices into the air fryer basket.
3. Cook salmon at 330 F for 15 minutes.
4. Meanwhile, in a bowl, mix together yogurt, garlic powder, lemon juice, dill, pepper, and salt.
5. Place salmon on serving plate and top with yogurt mixture.
6. Serve and enjoy.

Thai Shrimp

Preparation Time: 10 minutes
Cooking Time: 10 minutes
Serve: 4

Ingredients:

- 1 lb shrimp, peeled and deveined
- 1 tsp sesame seeds, toasted
- 2 garlic cloves, minced
- 2 tbsp soy sauce
- 2 tbsp Thai chili sauce
- 1 tbsp arrowroot powder
- 1 tbsp green onion, sliced
- 1/8 tsp ginger, minced

Directions:

1.Spray air fryer basket with cooking spray.
2.Toss shrimp with arrowroot powder and place into the air fryer basket.
3.Cook shrimp at 350 F for 5 minutes. Shake basket well and cook for 5 minutes more.
4.Meanwhile, in a bowl, mix together soy sauce, ginger, garlic, and chili sauce.
5.Add shrimp to the bowl and toss well.
6.Garnish with green onions and sesame seeds.
7.Serve and enjoy.

CHAPTER 6: MEATLESS MEALS RECIPES

Crispy Pickles

Preparation Time: 10 minutes
Cooking Time: 6 minutes
Serve: 4

Ingredients:

- 16 dill pickles, sliced
- 1 egg, lightly beaten
- 1/2 cup almond flour
- 3 tbsp parmesan cheese, grated
- 1/2 cup pork rind, crushed

Directions:

1. Take three bowls. Mix together pork rinds and cheese in the first bowl.
2. In a second bowl, add the egg.
3. In the last bowl add the almond flour.
4. Coat each pickle slice with almond flour then dip in egg and finally coat with pork and cheese mixture.
5. Spray air fryer basket with cooking spray.
6. Place coated pickles in the air fryer basket.
7. Cook pickles for 6 minutes at 370 F.
8. Serve and enjoy.

Spiced Green Beans

Preparation Time: 10 minutes
Cooking Time: 10 minutes
Serve: 2

Ingredients:

- 2 cups green beans
- 1/8 tsp cayenne pepper
- 1/8 tsp ground allspice
- 1/4 tsp ground cinnamon
- 1/2 tsp dried oregano
- 2 tbsp olive oil
- 1/4 tsp ground coriander
- 1/4 tsp ground cumin
- 1/2 tsp salt

Directions:

1.Add all ingredients into the large bowl and toss well.
2.Spray air fryer basket with cooking spray.
3.Add bowl mixture into the air fryer basket.
4.Cook at 370 F for 10 minutes. Shake basket halfway through
5.Serve and enjoy.

Roasted Carrots

Preparation Time: 10 minutes
Cooking Time: 25 minutes
Serve: 6

Ingredients:

- 16 small carrots
- 1 tbsp fresh parsley, chopped
- 1 tbsp dried basil
- 6 garlic cloves, minced
- 4 tbsp olive oil
- 1 1/2 tsp salt

Directions:

1. Preheat the air fryer to 350 F.
2. In a bowl, mix together oil, carrots, basil, garlic, and salt.
3. Transfer carrots into the air fryer basket and cook for 20-25 minutes. Shake basket 2-3 times while cooking.
4. Garnish with parsley and serve.

Mushroom Bean Casserole

Preparation Time: 10 minutes
Cooking Time: 12 minutes
Serve: 6

Ingredients:

- 2 cups mushrooms, sliced
- 1 tsp onion powder
- 1/2 tsp ground sage
- 1/2 tbsp garlic powder
- 1 fresh lemon juice
- 1 1/2 lbs green beans, trimmed
- 1/4 tsp pepper
- 1/2 tsp salt

Directions:

1. In a large mixing bowl, toss together green beans, onion powder, sage, garlic powder, lemon juice, mushrooms, pepper, and salt.
2. Spray air fryer basket with cooking spray.
3. Transfer green bean mixture into the air fryer basket.
4. Cook for 10-12 minutes at 400 F. Shake after every 3 minutes.
5. Serve and enjoy.

Asian Broccoli

Preparation Time: 10 minutes
Cooking Time: 20 minutes
Serve: 4

Ingredients:

- 1 lb broccoli, cut into florets
- 1 tsp rice vinegar
- 2 tsp sriracha
- 2 tbsp soy sauce
- 1 tbsp garlic, minced
- 5 drops liquid stevia
- 1 1/2 tbsp sesame oil
- Salt

Directions:

1. In a bowl, toss together broccoli, garlic, oil, and salt.
2. Spread broccoli in air fryer basket and cook for 15-20 minutes at 400 F.
3. Meanwhile, in a microwave-safe bowl mix together soy sauce, vinegar, liquid stevia, and sriracha and microwave for 10 seconds.
4. Transfer broccoli to a bowl and toss well with soy mixture to coat.
5. Serve and enjoy.

Quick Creamy Spinach

Preparation Time: 10 minutes
Cooking Time: 15 minutes
Serve: 2

Ingredients:

- 10 oz frozen spinach, thawed
- 1/4 cup parmesan cheese, shredded
- 1/2 tsp ground nutmeg
- 1 tsp pepper
- 4 oz cream cheese, diced
- 2 tsp garlic, minced
- 1 small onion, chopped
- 1 tsp salt

Directions:

1. Spray 6-inch pan with cooking spray and set aside.
2. In a bowl, mix together spinach, cream cheese, garlic, onion, nutmeg, pepper, and salt.
3. Pour spinach mixture into the prepared pan.
4. Place dish in air fryer basket and air fry at 350 F for 10 minutes.
5. Open air fryer basket and sprinkle parmesan cheese on top of spinach mixture and air fry at 400 F for 5 minutes more.
6. Serve and enjoy.

Ratatouille

Preparation Time: 10 minutes
Cooking Time: 25 minutes
Serve: 4

Ingredients:

- 1 tomato, cubed
- 1 zucchini, cubed
- 1/2 small eggplant, cubed
- 1 garlic clove, crushed
- 2 oregano sprigs, chopped
- 1 cayenne pepper, cubed
- 1/2 onion, cubed
- 1 bell pepper, cubed
- 1 tbsp vinegar
- 1 tbsp white wine
- 1 tbsp olive oil
- Pepper
- Salt

Directions:

1.Add all ingredients into the large mixing bowl and toss well.
2.Transfer vegetable mixture into the air fryer baking dish and place in the air fryer.
3.Cook at 400 F for 25 minutes. Stir after every 5 minutes.
4.Serve and enjoy.

Curried Sweet Potato Fries

Preparation Time: 10 minutes
Cooking Time: 20 minutes
Serve: 3

Ingredients:

- 2 sweet potatoes, peeled and cut into fries shape
- 1/4 tsp ground coriander
- 1/2 tsp curry powder
- 2 tbsp olive oil
- Pepper
- Salt

Directions:

1. Add all ingredients into the mixing bowl and toss to coat.
2. Transfer sweet potato fries into the air fryer basket and cook at 370 F for 20 minutes. Toss halfway through.
3. Serve and enjoy.

Curried Eggplant Slices

Preparation Time: 10 minutes
Cooking Time: 10 minutes
Serve: 2

Ingredients:

- 1 large eggplant, cut into 1/2-inch thick slices
- 1 garlic clove, minced
- 1 tbsp olive oil
- 1/2 tsp curry powder
- 1/8 tsp turmeric
- Salt

Directions:

1. Preheat the air fryer to 300 F.
2. Add all ingredients into the large mixing bowl and toss to coat.
3. Transfer eggplant slices into the air fryer basket.
4. Cook eggplant slices for 10 minutes or until lightly brown. Shake basket halfway through.
5. Serve and enjoy.

Squash Fritters

Preparation Time: 10 minutes
Cooking Time: 7 minutes
Serve: 4

Ingredients:

- 1 yellow summer squash, grated
- 1 egg, lightly beaten
- 3 oz cream cheese
- 2 tbsp olive oil
- 1/2 tsp dried oregano
- 1/4 cup almond flour
- 1/3 cup carrot, grated
- Pepper
- Salt

Directions:

1. Spray air fryer basket with cooking spray.
2. Add all ingredients into the mixing bowl and mix until well combined.
3. Make patties from bowl mixture and place into the air fryer basket and cook at 400 F for 7 minutes.
4. Serve and enjoy.

Tasty Okra

Preparation Time: 10 minutes
Cooking Time: 12 minutes
Serve: 2

Ingredients:

- 1/2 lb okra, ends trimmed and sliced
- 1 tsp olive oil
- 1/2 tsp mango powder
- 1/2 tsp chili powder
- 1/2 tsp ground coriander
- 1/2 tsp ground cumin
- 1/8 tsp pepper
- 1/4 tsp salt

Directions:

1.Preheat the air fryer to 350 F.
2.Add all ingredients into the large bowl and toss well.
3.Spray air fryer basket with cooking spray.
4.Transfer okra mixture into the air fryer basket and cook for 10 minutes. Shake basket halfway through.
5.Toss okra well and cook for 2 minutes more.
6.Serve and enjoy.

Cauliflower Rice

Preparation Time: 10 minutes
Cooking Time: 12 minutes
Serve: 3

Ingredients:

- 1 cauliflower head, cut into florets
- 2 tbsp olive oil
- 2 garlic cloves, chopped
- 1 tomato, chopped
- 1 onion, chopped
- 2 tbsp tomato paste
- 1 tsp white pepper
- 1 tsp pepper
- 1 tbsp dried thyme
- 2 chilies, chopped
- 1/2 tsp salt

Directions:

1. Preheat the air fryer to 370 F.
2. Add cauliflower florets into the food processor and process until it looks like rice.
3. Stir in tomato paste, tomatoes, and spices and mix well.
4. Add cauliflower mixture into the air fryer baking pan and drizzle with olive oil.
5. Place pan in the air fryer and cook for 12 minutes.
6. Serve and enjoy.

Ricotta Mushrooms

Preparation Time: 10 minutes
Cooking Time: 12 minutes
Serve: 4

Ingredients:

- 4 large Portobello mushrooms caps
- 1 tbsp olive oil
- 1/4 cup parmesan cheese, grated
- 1/4 tsp rosemary, chopped
- 1 cup spinach, chopped
- 1/4 cup ricotta cheese

Directions:

1. Coat mushrooms with olive oil.
2. Transfer mushrooms into the air fryer basket and cook at 350 F for 2 minutes.
3. In a bowl, mix together remaining ingredients.
4. Stuff bowl mixture into the mushrooms and place into the air fryer basket and cook for 10 minutes more.
5. Serve and enjoy.

Spicy Buffalo Cauliflower

Preparation Time: 10 minutes
Cooking Time: 15 minutes
Serve: 4

Ingredients:

- 8 oz cauliflower florets
- 1 tsp cayenne pepper
- 1 tsp chili powder
- 1 tsp olive oil
- 1 tsp garlic, minced
- 1 tomato, diced
- 6 tbsp almond flour
- 1 tsp black pepper
- 1/2 tsp salt

Directions:

1. Preheat the air fryer to 350 F.
2. Spray air fryer basket with cooking spray.
3. Add tomato, garlic, black pepper, olive oil, cayenne pepper, and chili powder into the blender and blend until smooth.
4. Add cauliflower florets into the bowl. Season with pepper and salt.
5. Pour blended mixture over cauliflower florets and toss well to coat.
6. Coat cauliflower florets with almond flour and place into the air fryer basket and cook for 15 minutes. Shake basket 2-3 times.
7. Serve and enjoy.

-

CHAPTER 7: DESSERTS RECIPES

Crustless Pie

Preparation Time: 10 minutes
Cooking Time: 24 minutes
Serve: 4

Ingredients:

- 3 eggs
- 1/2 cup pumpkin puree
- 1/2 tsp cinnamon
- 1 tsp vanilla
- 1/4 cup erythritol
- 1/2 cup cream
- 1/2 cup unsweetened almond milk

Directions:

1. Preheat the air fryer to 325 F.
2. Spray air fryer baking dish with cooking spray and set aside.
3. In a large bowl, add all ingredients and beat until smooth.
4. Pour pie mixture into the prepared dish and place into the air fryer and cook for 24 minutes.
5. Let it cool completely and place into the refrigerator for 1-2 hours.
6. Slice and serve.

Cappuccino Muffins

Preparation Time: 10 minutes
Cooking Time: 20 minutes
Serve: 12

Ingredients:

- 4 eggs
- 2 cups almond flour
- 1/2 tsp vanilla
- 1 tsp espresso powder
- 1/2 cup sour cream
- 1 tsp cinnamon
- 2 tsp baking powder
- 1/4 cup coconut flour
- 1/2 cup Swerve
- 1/4 tsp salt

Directions:

1. Preheat the air fryer to 325 F.
2. Add sour cream, vanilla, espresso powder, and eggs in a blender and blend until smooth.
3. Add almond flour, cinnamon, baking powder, coconut flour, sweetener, and salt. Blend again until smooth.
4. Pour batter into the silicone muffin molds and place into the air fryer basket. (Cook in batches)
5. Cook muffins for 20 minutes.
6. Serve and enjoy.

Almond Coconut Lemon Cake

Preparation Time: 10 minutes
Cooking Time: 48 minutes
Serve: 10

Ingredients:

- 4 eggs
- 2 tbsp lemon zest
- 1/2 cup butter softened
- 2 tsp baking powder
- 1/4 cup coconut flour
- 2 cups almond flour
- 1/2 cup fresh lemon juice
- 1/4 cup swerve
- 1 tbsp vanilla

Directions:

1. Preheat the air fryer to 280 F.
2. Spray air fryer baking dish with cooking spray and set aside.
3. In a large bowl, beat all ingredients using a hand mixer until a smooth.
4. Pour batter into the prepared dish and place into the air fryer and cook for 48 minutes.
5. Slice and serve.

Cinnamon Pecan Muffins

Preparation Time: 10 minutes
Cooking Time: 15 minutes
Serve: 12

Ingredients:

- 4 eggs
- 1 1/2 cups almond flour
- 1 tsp vanilla
- 1/4 cup unsweetened almond milk
- 2 tbsp butter, melted
- 1/2 cup erythritol
- 1 tsp psyllium husk
- 1/2 cup pecans, chopped
- 1/2 tsp ground cinnamon
- 2 tsp allspice
- 1 tbsp baking powder

Directions:

1. Preheat the air fryer to 400 F.
2. Beat eggs, milk, vanilla, sweetener, and butter in a bowl using a hand mixer until smooth.
3. Add remaining ingredients and stir until combined.
4. Pour batter into silicone muffin molds and place in the air fryer. In batches.
5. Cook for 15 minutes.
6. Serve and enjoy.

Tasty Peanut Butter Bars

Preparation Time: 10 minutes
Cooking Time: 24 minutes
Serve: 9

Ingredients:

- 2 eggs
- 1 tbsp coconut flour
- 1/2 cup butter, softened
- 1/2 cup peanut butter
- 1/4 cup almond flour
- 1/2 cup swerve

Directions:

1.Spray air fryer baking pan with cooking spray and set aside.
2.In a bowl, beat together butter, eggs, and peanut butter until well combined.
3.Add dry ingredients and mix until a smooth batter is formed.
4.Spread batter evenly in prepared pan and place into the air fryer and cook at 325 F for 24 minutes.
5.Slice and serve.

Egg Custard

Preparation Time: 10 minutes
Cooking Time: 32 minutes
Serve: 6

Ingredients:

- 2 egg yolks
- 3 eggs
- 1/2 cup erythritol
- 2 cups heavy whipping cream
- 1/2 tsp vanilla
- 1 tsp nutmeg

Directions:

1.Preheat the air fryer to 325 F.
2.Add all ingredients into the large bowl and beat until well combined.
3.Pour custard mixture into the greased baking dish and place into the air fryer.
4.Cook for 32 minutes.
5.Let it cool completely then place in the refrigerator for 1-2 hours.
6.Serve and enjoy.

Apple Chips with Dip

Preparation Time: 10 minutes
Cooking Time: 12 minutes
Serve: 4

Ingredients:

- 1 apple, thinly slice using a mandolin slicer
- 1 tbsp almond butter
- 1/4 cup plain yogurt
- 2 tsp olive oil
- 1 tsp ground cinnamon
- 4 drops liquid stevia

Directions:

1. Add apple slices, oil, and cinnamon in a large bowl and toss well.
2. Spray air fryer basket with cooking spray.
3. Place apple slices in air fryer basket and cook at 375 F for 12 minutes. Turn after every 4 minutes.
4. Meanwhile, in a small bowl, mix together almond butter, yogurt, and sweetener.
5. Serve apple chips with dip and enjoy.

Tasty Cheese Bites

Preparation Time: 10 minutes
Cooking Time: 2 minutes
Serve: 16

Ingredients:

- 8 oz cream cheese, softened
- 2 tbsp erythritol
- 1/2 cup almond flour
- 1/2 tsp vanilla
- 4 tbsp heavy cream
- 1/2 cup erythritol

Directions:

1. Add cream cheese, vanilla, 1/2 cup erythritol, and 2 tbsp heavy cream in a stand mixer and mix until smooth.
2. Scoop cream cheese mixture onto the parchment lined plate and place in the refrigerator for 1 hour.
3. In a small bowl, mix together almond flour and 2 tbsp erythritol.
4. Dip cheesecake bites in remaining heavy cream and coat with almond flour mixture.
5. Place prepared cheesecake bites in air fryer basket and air fry for 2 minutes at 350 F.
6. Make sure cheesecake bites are frozen before air fry otherwise they will melt.
7. Drizzle with chocolate syrup and serve.

Pecan Muffins

Preparation Time: 10 minutes
Cooking Time: 15 minutes
Serve: 12

Ingredients:

- 4 eggs
- 1 tsp vanilla
- 1/4 cup almond milk
- 2 tbsp butter, melted
- 1/2 cup swerve
- 1 tsp psyllium husk
- 1 tbsp baking powder
- 1/2 cup pecans, chopped
- 1/2 tsp ground cinnamon
- 2 tsp allspice
- 1 1/2 cups almond flour

Directions:

1. Preheat the air fryer to 370 F.
2. Beat eggs, almond milk, vanilla, sweetener, and butter in a bowl using a hand mixer until smooth.
3. Add remaining ingredients and mix until well combined.
4. Pour batter into the silicone muffin molds and place into the air fryer basket in batches.
5. Cook muffins for 15 minutes.
6. Serve and enjoy.

Cinnamon Ginger Cookies

Preparation Time: 10 minutes
Cooking Time: 12 minutes
Serve: 8

Ingredients:

- 1 egg
- 1/2 tsp vanilla
- 1/8 tsp ground cloves
- 1 tsp baking powder
- 3/4 cup erythritol
- 2/4 cup butter, melted
- 1 1/2 cups almond flour
- 1/4 tsp ground nutmeg
- 1/4 tsp ground cinnamon
- 1/2 tsp ground ginger
- Pinch of salt

Directions:

1. In a large bowl, mix together all dry ingredients.
2. In a separate bowl, mix together all wet ingredients.
3. Add dry ingredients to the wet ingredients and mix until dough is formed. Cover and place in the fridge for 30 minutes.
4. Preheat the air fryer to 325 F.
5. Make cookies from dough and place into the air fryer and cook for 12 minutes.
6. Serve and enjoy.

Pumpkin Cookies

Preparation Time: 10 minutes
Cooking Time: 20 minutes
Serve: 27

Ingredients:

- 1 egg
- 2 cups almond flour
- 1/2 tsp baking powder
- 1 tsp vanilla
- 1/2 cup butter
- 15 drops liquid stevia
- 1/2 tsp pumpkin pie spice
- 1/2 cup pumpkin puree

Directions:

1.Preheat the air fryer to 280 F.
2.In a large bowl, add all ingredients and mix until well combined.
3.Make cookies from mixture and place into the air fryer and cook for 20 minutes.
4.Serve and enjoy.

Blueberry Muffins

Preparation Time: 10 minutes
Cooking Time: 20 minutes
Serve: 12

Ingredients:

- 3 large eggs
- 1/3 cup coconut oil, melted
- 1 1/2 tsp gluten-free baking powder
- 1/2 cup erythritol
- 2 1/2 cups almond flour
- 3/4 cup blueberries
- 1/2 tsp vanilla
- 1/3 cup unsweetened almond milk

Directions:

1. Preheat the air fryer to 325 F.
2. In a large bowl, stir together almond flour, baking powder, erythritol.
3. Mix in the coconut oil, vanilla, eggs, and almond milk. Add blueberries and fold well.
4. Pour batter into the silicone muffin molds and place into the air fryer basket in batches.
5. Cook muffins for 20 minutes.
6. Serve and enjoy.

Easy Lava Cake

Preparation Time: 10 minutes
Cooking Time: 9 minutes
Serve: 2

Ingredients:

- 1 egg
- 1/2 tsp baking powder
- 1 tbsp coconut oil, melted
- 1 tbsp flax meal
- 2 tbsp erythritol
- 2 tbsp water
- 2 tbsp unsweetened cocoa powder
- Pinch of salt

Directions:

1.Whisk all ingredients into the bowl and transfer in two ramekins.
2.Preheat the air fryer to 350 F.
3.Place ramekins in air fryer basket and bake for 8-9 minutes.
4.Carefully remove ramekins from air fryer and let it cool for 10 minutes.
5.Serve and enjoy.

Vanilla Coconut Cheese Cookies

Preparation Time: 10 minutes
Cooking Time: 12 minutes
Serve: 15

Ingredients:

- 1 egg
- 1/2 tsp baking powder
- 1 tsp vanilla
- 1/2 cup swerve
- 1/2 cup butter, softened
- 3 tbsp cream cheese, softened
- 1/2 cup coconut flour
- Pinch of salt

Directions:

1. In a bowl, beat together butter, sweetener, and cream cheese.
2. Add egg and vanilla and beat until smooth and creamy.
3. Add coconut flour, salt, and baking powder and beat until combined. Cover and place in the fridge for 1 hour.
4. Preheat the air fryer to 325 F.
5. Make cookies from dough and place into the air fryer and cook for 12 minutes.
6. Serve and enjoy.

-

CONCLUSION

This excellent cookbook not only contains 1001-Day Delicious, Gut-Friendly Recipes that you can make right in Low-Fodmap Air Fryer in just a matter of minutes, but also the secrets to unlocking the air fryer's true potential that few people use! No more improvising with Low-Fodmap Air Fryer, no more using obsolete recipes.

Now you can save time, money, and start eating healthier versions of your favorite foods using your oven's full power, thanks to this revolutionary cookbook!

Stop wasting your time trying to find delicious and healthy recipes. Grab a copy of this cookbook and start enjoying the crunch without the calories and messy cleanup with Low-Fodmap Air Fryer Cookbook for Beginners! Get more about Low-Fodmap Diet with Low-Fodmap Air Fryer.

CPSIA information can be obtained
at www.ICGtesting.com
Printed in the USA
LVHW110750120122
708377LV00019B/907